anythink

D0577188

Fascinating INSECTS

Praying Mantises

Aaron Carr

LET'S READ

AV²
BY WEIGL™

ADDED VALUE • AUDIO VISUAL

www.av2books.com

Go to www.av2books.com, and enter this book's unique code.

BOOK CODE

F704765

AV² by Weigl brings you media enhanced books that support active learning.

AV² provides enriched content that supplements and complements this book. Weigl's AV² books strive to create inspired learning and engage young minds in a total learning experience.

Your AV² Media Enhanced books come alive with...

Audio
Listen to sections of the book read aloud.

Video
Watch informative video clips.

Embedded Weblinks
Gain additional information for research.

Try This!
Complete activities and hands-on experiments.

Key Words
Study vocabulary, and complete a matching word activity.

Quizzes
Test your knowledge.

Slide Show
View images and captions, and prepare a presentation.

... and much, much more!

Published by AV² by Weigl
350 5ᵗʰ Avenue, 59ᵗʰ Floor, New York, NY 10118
Website: www.av2books.com   www.weigl.com

Library of Congress Control Number: 2013937274
ISBN 978-1-62127-329-5 (hardcover)
ISBN 978-1-62127-334-9 (softcover)

Printed in the United States of America in North Mankato, Minnesota
1 2 3 4 5 6 7 8 9 0   17 16 15 14 13

052013
WEP040413

Project Coordinator: Aaron Carr   Art Director: Terry Paulhus

Weigl acknowledges Getty Images as the primary image supplier for this title.

Praying Mantises

CONTENTS

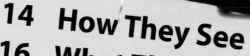

2 AV² Book Code
4 Meet the Praying Mantis
6 Where They Live
8 Life Cycle
10 Name
12 Wings
14 How They See
16 What They Eat
18 How They Hunt
20 Role on Farms
22 Praying Mantis Facts
24 Key Words

Meet the praying mantis.

The praying mantis is a large insect.
It is one of the largest insects
in the world.

6

The praying mantis lives
in most parts of the world.

In most parts of the world,
the mantis lives on plants.

7

The praying mantis hatches
from an egg when it is born.

When it is born, the mantis is small and white.

The praying mantis
holds its front legs together.

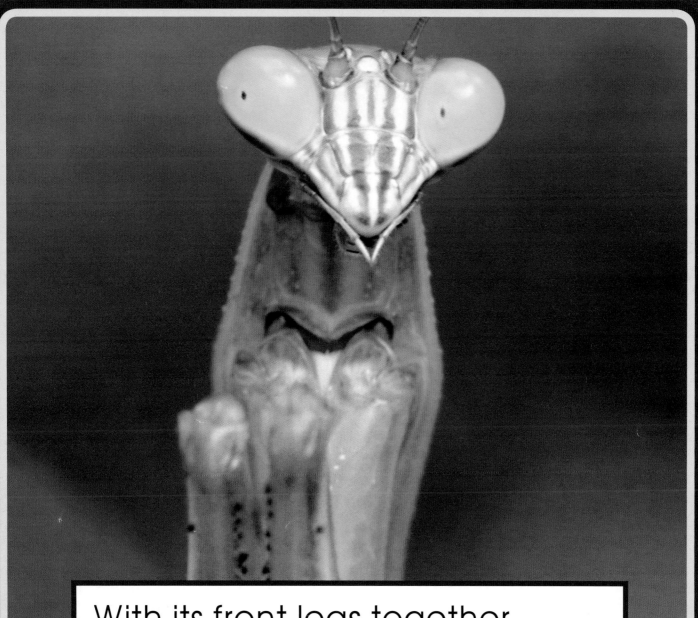

With its front legs together,
it looks like the mantis is praying.

The praying mantis
has two sets of wings.

With two sets of wings, the mantis can scare away bigger animals.

The praying mantis has five eyes.

With five eyes,
the mantis can find its food.

The praying mantis eats insects.

Eating insects gives the mantis everything it needs to be healthy.

The praying mantis hunts by hiding on plants.

By hiding on plants, the mantis can catch its food by surprise.

The praying mantis
is sometimes kept on farms.

On farms, the mantis eats pests
that feed on crops.

21

PRAYING MANTIS FACTS

These pages provide more detail about the interesting facts found in the book. They are intended to be used by adults as a learning support to help young readers round out their knowledge of each insect or arachnid featured in the *Fascinating Insects* series.

Pages 4–5

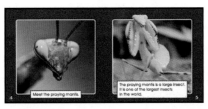

Praying mantises are large insects. They have six jointed legs and bodies with three parts: the head, thorax, and abdomen. Insects have hard outer shells called exoskeletons. There are about 2,000 species in the mantis family. Also known as mantids, they are among the largest insects in the world. The largest mantids can be up to 6 inches (15 centimeters) long. The smallest mantids are only 0.5 inches (1.2 cm) in length.

Pages 6–7

Praying mantises live in most parts of the world. Mantises are found on all continents except Antarctica. They mostly live in warm tropical or subtropical areas. Mantises live in forests, gardens, or other areas with abundant plant life. They spend most of their time on plants. Their green and brown coloring helps them blend in with plants.

Pages 8–9

Praying mantises hatch from eggs when they are born. Mantises lay up to 400 eggs each fall. They attach the eggs to plants in a protective covering, called an ootheca. After hatching, the mantis is in its nymph stage. Nymphs look like very small mantises without wings. The nymphs grow throughout summer. By fall, they have reached full size and grown their wings.

Pages 10–11

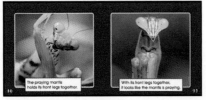

Praying mantises hold their front legs together. The praying mantis is named for its front legs, which have adapted to be used like arms. These legs are larger and more powerful than the other legs. The mantis often holds its front legs folded and angled to touch at the ends. This is similar to how a person holds his or her hands when praying. The name mantis comes from the Greek word for "prophet."

Pages 12–13

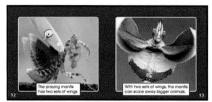

Praying mantises have two sets of wings. However, not all species of mantis have wings, and many winged species cannot fly. Instead, these mantises use their wings to defend themselves from predators. If a predator approaches, the mantis will raise and flap its wings to make itself appear larger. Some mantises have spots on their wings that look like large eyes.

Pages 14–15

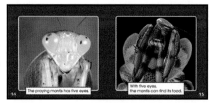

Praying mantises have five eyes. They have exceptional eyesight compared to other insects. The mantis has two large compound eyes on each side of its head. With these eyes, the mantis can see objects about 50 feet (15 meters) away. It also has three simple eyes in the center of its forehead. These eyes can only see differences between light and dark. The mantis can turn its head 180 degrees. This helps the mantis scan its environment for food.

Pages 16–17

Praying mantises eat insects. They are carnivores, which means they hunt other animals for food. Mantises usually eat small insects such as moths, crickets, grasshoppers, and flies. However, the praying mantis has also been known to eat small animals, including frogs, lizards, mice, and hummingbirds. The mantis has a row of spikes along the insides of its front legs. These spikes help the mantis grab and hold on to its prey.

Pages 18–19

Praying mantises hunt by hiding on plants. Mantises use stealth and camouflage to hunt their prey. They will sit still on plant stems or leaves that match their body color. This helps them avoid being seen by their prey. When prey come close, the mantis grabs the prey with its large front legs. This takes the mantis about one-twentieth of a second, which is too fast for people to see.

Pages 20–21

Praying mantises are sometimes kept on farms. Mantises are welcomed by most farmers and gardeners. This is because mantises prey on many insects that are considered pests. Many farmers even purchase mantises to serve as a natural form of pest control. However, some insects reproduce too quickly for mantises to control. Farmers must also consider that the praying mantis will eat nearly all of the insects it finds, including those that have a positive impact on crops.

KEY WORDS

Research has shown that as much as 65 percent of all written material published in English is made up of 300 words. These 300 words cannot be taught using pictures or learned by sounding them out. They must be recognized by sight. This book contains 43 common sight words to help young readers improve their reading fluency and comprehension. This book also teaches young readers several important content words. These words are paired with pictures to aid in learning and improve understanding.

Page	Sight Words First Appearance
4	the
5	a, in, is, it, large, of, one, world
7	lives, most, on, parts, plants
8	an, from, when
9	and, small, white
10	its, together
11	like, looks, with
12	has, sets, two
13	animals, away, can
14	eyes
15	find, food
17	be, eats, gives, needs, to
18	by
20	farms, sometimes, that

Page	Content Words First Appearance
4	praying mantis
5	insect
8	egg
10	legs
12	wings
20	crops, pests

Check out www.av2books.com for activities, videos, audio clips, and more!

1 Go to www.av2books.com.

2 Enter book code. **F 7 0 4 7 6 5**

3 Fuel your imagination online!

www.av2books.com